FROM THIS
DAY FORWARD

Also by Craig Groeschel

Altar Ego: Becoming Who God Says You Are

Chazown: A Different Way to See Your Life

The Christian Atheist:
Believing in God but Living as If He Doesn't Exist

Daring to Drop the Pose
(previously titled *Confessions of a Pastor*)

Fight: Winning the Battles That Matter Most

God, Love, and Sex
(previously titled *Going All the Way*)

It: How Churches and Leaders Can Get It and Keep It

Soul Detox: Pure Living in a Polluted World

Weird: Because Normal Isn't Working

What Is God Really Like? (general editor)

FROM THIS DAY FORWARD

Five Commitments to Fail-Proof Your Marriage

CRAIG AND AMY GROESCHEL

with Kevin and Sherry Harney

ZONDERVAN

From This Day Forward Study Guide
Copyright © 2014 by Craig Groeschel

This title is also available as a Zondervan ebook.
Visit www.zondervan.com/ebooks.

Requests for information should be addressed to:

Zondervan, 3900 *Sparks Dr. SE, Grand Rapids, Michigan 49546*

ISBN 978-0-310-69719-0

All Scripture quotations, unless otherwise indicated, are taken from The Holy Bible, *New International Version®, NIV®.* Copyright © 1973, 1978, 1984, 2011 by Biblica, Inc.® Used by permission. All rights reserved worldwide.

Any Internet addresses (websites, blogs, etc.) and telephone numbers in this book are offered as a resource. They are not intended in any way to be or imply an endorsement by Zondervan, nor does Zondervan vouch for the content of these sites and numbers for the life of this book.

Craig Groeschel is represented by Thomas J. Winters and Jeffrey C. Dunn of Winters, King & Associates, Inc., Tulsa, Oklahoma.

Cover design: Curt Diepenhorst
Cover photography: Michelle Meisner

First Printing August 2014 / Printed in the United States of America

Contents

Of Note

The quotations interspersed throughout this study guide, the introductory comments, and the concluding comments are excerpts from the book *From This Day Forward* and the video curriculum of the same name by Craig and Amy Groeschel. All other resources — including the small group questions, session introductions, and between-sessions materials — have been written by Kevin and Sherry Harney in collaboration with Craig and Amy Groeschel.

HOW TO USE THIS GUIDE

GROUP SIZE

The *From This Day Forward* curriculum is designed to be experienced in a group setting such as a Bible study, Sunday school class, or any small group gathering. To ensure everyone has enough time to participate in discussion and exercises, it is recommended that larger groups break up into smaller groups of six to eight people.

MATERIALS NEEDED

Even though this is a study geared to married couples, ideally each participant should have his or her own group study guide. This guide provides notes for video segments, directions for activities, discussion questions, space to journal, and ideas for personal reflection and learning between group sessions. You will gain the full benefit of this learning experience by interacting with the materials in this small group guide.

TIMING

The time notations indicate the actual time of video segments and also the suggested times for interaction, activities, and discussion. If you follow the suggested time allotted for each portion of the study, you will conclude in approximately one hour. If you have a longer meeting time, you might want to allow more space for discussion, interaction, and group prayer.

If your group wants to slow down and go deeper, you might want to spend two weeks on each session. This pace works well for a group meeting for one quarter of the year. If you do this, it also makes it easier to follow along and read the book *From This Day Forward* as a couple while you are walking through the small group experience.

FACILITATION

If you do not have a set group leader, each group should appoint a facilitator who is responsible for starting the video and for keeping track of the time during discussions and activities. Facilitators may also read questions aloud and monitor discussions, prompting group members to respond and ensuring that everyone has the opportunity to participate.

PERSONAL STUDIES

Maximize the impact of the curriculum with further study between the group sessions. Every week there are additional resources such as personal reflection questions, Bible study, prayer direction, reading assignments from the *From This Day Forward* book, and other creative activities. You will get the most out of this group learning experience and strengthen your marriage in greater measure by setting aside one hour between your group gatherings for personal study.

INTRODUCTION

My wife, Amy, and I don't have a perfect marriage — far from it. But we love each other more now than when we said "I do" more than twenty-three years (and six kids) ago. We've discovered that the key to a successful marriage is something you've heard before. But you may not have thought about what it means. Your key to a joyful, life-giving marriage begins with you completely understanding this one simple phrase: "I, [your name here], take you, [your spouse's name here], to have and to hold, *from this day forward.*"

Those four little words are packed full of hope, brimming with promise: "From this day forward."

What happened in your past doesn't matter. Did you mess up when you were dating? That's okay! Have you struggled with communicating? That's okay! Have you said things you wish you could take back? That's okay! Have you done things you regret? *It's okay.* God's mercies, his compassions, never fail. They are new every morning. And he is always faithful (Lamentations 3:22 – 23).

Draw a line today. Your new lifelong love life, your new love affair with each other, the greatest marriage you can imagine, begins now. Today. From this day forward. Right now, in this very moment, you can commit that everything that happens from now on will represent your sacred commitment to your spouse before a holy God.

From this day forward.

A lot of people seem to ignore the fact that, if you've chosen to follow Christ, regardless of whether it was before or after you slipped that ring onto that special someone's finger, it's a commitment you make before God. It's easy to excuse our own behavior — our mistakes and bad habits — when we compare our shortcomings with our spouse's. But for those of us who call ourselves Christians, that's not really our standard, is it?

We say, "I take you for better or for worse, for richer or for poorer, in sickness and in health, and forsaking all others, I will be faithful to you for as long as we both shall live, *so help me, God.*"

We need to allow God to take his rightful place in our relationships. We acknowledge our weaknesses, admitting that we know it's impossible for us to keep our commitments unless we choose to honor him at the very center of our marriage (2 Corinthians 12:9).

Our commitments are based on decisions. The choices you make each and every day determine not only your relationship with God but also the quality of your marriage. The decisions you make *today* determine the marriage you will have *tomorrow*. If you make these decisions, you can and will have the marriage God wants you to experience.

If you and your spouse (or future spouse) earnestly choose to do all five of these things discussed in this five-session study, we promise you'll discover a richer, deeper, more authentic, more rewarding, more passionate love life than the greatest fantasy your teenage self ever could have imagined.

Don't be a statistic. Don't be average. Let's get you that marriage that you always wanted. Starting right now, from this day forward.

Trusting and believing God has great plans for your marriage,

Craig and Amy

Session 1

SEEK GOD

*Our first priority in life
is not seeking a spouse ...
it is seeking God.*

WHO IS REALLY NUMBER ONE? (2 – 3 MINUTES)

If you hang around the church, even for a little while, you will hear the famous words of Jesus about the greatest commandment in the entire Bible. When Jesus walked on this earth, the religious leaders of his day kept trying to get him to say something wrong so they could accuse him of false beliefs and turn the crowds against him.

On one of these occasions, a group of high-level religious professionals came and asked Jesus, "Which is the greatest commandment in the law?" (Matthew 22:36). Jesus replied with confidence and passion, "Love the Lord your God with all your heart and with all your soul and with all your mind" (v. 37). Then the Savior went on to explain that this is the most important commandment, and second on the list is to "love your neighbor as yourself" (v. 39).

In simple terms, Jesus was saying, "Make God number one in your heart and life. Everyone else, and everything else, should come in second, third, or farther down the list." The whole Bible rings loud and clear with this message. Put God first, seek him before all else, and let nothing else take the central place in your life that only God deserves.

If you ask most Christians if God is really number one in their heart and life, they will say a quick and emphatic *yes*! But we should all slow down and take a good look at our schedule, finances, priorities, and earthly relationships. Is God really first? Do we seek him before all else and above all else?

> *Our marriage will never be what God wants it to be unless he is One and our spouse is two.*

There is a biblical word that describes the reality that settles into our lives when another person (or thing) begins to come before God in our heart, schedule, and devotion. The word is *idolatry*. All through the Bible God is clear that this is one of the biggest sins and pitfalls that his people will ever face. As a matter of fact, idolatry is so prevalent and the temptation to commit it is so great that the first two of the Ten Commandments (Exodus 20:3 – 6) address this issue:

COMMANDMENT 1: "You shall have no other gods before me."

COMMANDMENT 2: "You shall not make for yourself an image in the form of anything …"

God knows that if we put him first, love him most, and follow him above all, every other relationship in our life will be better, stronger, and built on a firm foundation. This includes a marriage. When we seek God first, he will prepare us and help us to be the spouse we are meant to me.

So, how are you doing? Don't answer too quickly!

Is God first in your life? Is he truly number one?

TALK ABOUT IT (4 – 5 MINUTES)

If this is a new group, give your name and briefly mention one thing you are hoping to learn or experience during this study. Then answer the following question:

When a couple is talking about getting married, lots of people are eager to share advice. Tell about a time you heard someone say something discouraging about marriage. Or, tell about a time someone gave helpful, hopeful, and valuable advice and words about marriage.

> *If you want to have a godly marriage one day, live a godly life today!*

VIDEO TEACHING NOTES (18 MINUTES)

As you watch the video teaching segment for session 1, use the following outline to follow along or to record anything that stands out to you.

Two views of marriage:

1. The world, and even some Christians, discourages marriage and focuses on the fact that it is hard and challenging.

2. God invented marriage and wants us to know that it can be an amazing gift and that there is hope for your marriage. God can heal even the most broken and challenging marriage.

Statistics show that 50 percent of marriages don't make it. This can dishearten and discourage us. Or we can determine that we will approach marriage from a different perspective and make specific and serious commitments to build a healthy, lasting, God-honoring marriage.

Rather than just hoping for the best, we can make five commitments that will help us develop the kind of marriage we long to have. These commitments are:

- Seek God.
- Fight fair.

- Have fun.
- Stay pure.
- Never give up.

In many wedding ceremonies the couple will say the words, "From this day forward." This declaration and attitude brings a hope-filled perspective that honors God. We can be confident that if we take the right steps, make the right decisions, and engage in actions that are biblical and consistent with God's design, things can begin to get better "from this day forward."

Seeking God

Many people are not seeking God ... they are seeking a spouse.

Looking for **The One!** Often we are looking for that perfect person who will meet our needs, make us whole, and bring us ultimate joy and meaning. But this is dangerous and built on a false idea.

Let God be **Your One** and your spouse be **Your two!** The only way a marriage will be truly healthy and happy is if we get these things in the right order.

Jesus replied: " 'Love the Lord your God with all your heart and with all your soul and with all your mind.' This is the first and greatest commandment. And the second is like it: 'Love your neighbor as yourself.' All the Law and the Prophets hang on these two commandments" (Matthew 22:37 – 40).

Words to those who are not yet married . . .

A wise declaration and commitment: "I will seek the One while preparing for my two."

When a person is not yet married, their greatest goal and desire should be to seek, honor, follow, and grow in love with God.

"But seek first his kingdom and his righteousness, and all these things will be given to you as well" (Matthew 6:33).

A dangerous mindset . . . putting off "the God thing" until we find a spouse and then trying to get things right with God.

Words to those who are married . . .

A wise declaration and commitment: "I will always seek the One with my two."

We make a dangerous mistake when we let anything else become our one and put God in the second place. This includes our spouse, kids, career, or anything else in life.

When we let anyone or anything take first place in our life, before God, there is a word for this: *idolatry*!

When we put a person in first place in our life and heart, we place undue and unrealistic pressure on them which they can never fulfill.

Finally, when we idolize a person and they let us down (and they always will), then we demonize them.

Craig and Amy ... Seeking the One with Your Two

Understand the critical role of a husband giving leadership in the relationship.

Be natural in how you seek God as a couple.

Many men feel unprepared or uncomfortable taking leadership in this area of the relationship.

A keystone habit to get you started: **Pray together every day.**

- It can be short and focused.
- It should be natural.
- It should not be a formula.
- It can be anywhere.
- It can be anytime.
- It can be a specific time.

- It grows our humility.
- It builds unity.

In any area of life, if we knew there was a 50 percent chance of experiencing failure, we would make significant adjustments to do all we can to succeed.

VIDEO DISCUSSION AND BIBLE EXPLORATION

(25 – 30 MINUTES)

1. Name some of the things (or people) that can take first place in our heart in the following seasons of life:

- When we are children
- In our teenage years
- In the college and early adult years
- In the early years of marriage (when young children are often in the picture)
- In our middle-age years
- In the later years of life

Describe why putting this thing or person first can be unhealthy and how it could hurt our relationship with God.

2. Tell about a person you know who really puts God first, seeks him passionately, and keeps Jesus in the center of their life. How has this person's commitment to seek God first impacted the rest of their relationships? If they are married, how has their devotion to make God number one in life impacted their marriage relationship?

> *Be the kind of person you would like to marry.*

3. God loves to give us fresh new beginnings, and his mercy is endless (Lamentations 3:22 – 23). Craig and Amy suggest that you can have a new start in your marriage today, "from this day forward." How can this attitude help set the tone for the rest of your married life? Why is it important to forgive and leave some things in the past as we press forward into a new future?

4. What are some of the ways our culture and the media propel people toward the idea that life is about finding "The One" perfect person who will meet our needs, make us whole, and lead us to pure happiness? What are some of the dangers and possible consequences of viewing a spouse (or potential spouse) as "The One"?

> *It does not matter how bad or mediocre a marriage is. "From this day forward," God can lead you toward a better marriage.*

5. **Read:** Matthew 22:34 – 40. If God is going to be our "One," we will need to love him with everything in us. What are specific and practical ways we can do so with our whole heart, soul, and mind?

6. When a husband or wife is growing in their love for God (their "One") each day and putting God first in their life, how can this

impact the way they interact with their spouse (their "two") in any of the following situations:

☐ When they have a disagreement over a decision or life situation

☐ When there has been a breech in trust or a deep hurt between them

☐ When the couple faces a loss or time of pain together

☐ When their spouse does not care for them the way they hoped or dreamed they would

☐ When a spouse becomes ill or faces a time when they can't offer a lot or fulfill some of the normal marital responsibilities

☐ Make up your own scenario ...

7. What are some specific and practical ways a married couple can "Seek the One with their two"? Work as a group to form a list of at least eight ways a married couple can grow in their faith together.

   •

   •

   •

-
-
-
-
-
-

Satan would like nothing better than for none of us ever to seek God—not on our own, and certainly not with our two.

8. In the video, Craig talks about how making a person our "One" puts undue and unrealistic expectations on them. If we look to a spouse to meet all of our needs, make us happy, and fulfill our dreams, what are some of the possible negative consequences this will have on our marriage relationship?

9. The danger of idolizing our spouse is that when they let us down, we will begin to demonize them. Craig gave a couple of examples of how this can happen. Add to the list and talk about others ways husbands and wives can make a shift in how they see each other.

Idolize	Demonize
He is so relaxed, easygoing, and free spirited ... I love it!	He is lazy, unmotivated, and plays too many video games ... he needs to work harder.
She knows what she believes, expresses it, and holds to her convictions ... I respect that.	She is controlling, domineering, and is always trying to make me do things her way ... it bugs me!

10. Tell about your journey of praying together as a couple. Then try to come up with one way the two of you can take a step deeper into prayer and how your group members can cheer you on and encourage you to grow in this discipline.

The hardest part about learning to pray together is ... starting!

CLOSING PRAYER (5 – 10 MINUTES)

Take time as a group to pray in any of the following directions:

- Thank Jesus for being so clear that loving God with all that you are should be the first priority in your life. Ask him to help you grow to love him even more.

- Invite the Holy Spirit to show you any place in your life where someone or something is becoming an idol. Ask for power to cast down this idol and put God first.

- Pray for each couple represented in your group to learn how to seek God first as they learn to put each other second.

- Lift up young people you care about (your own children if you have them), and pray that they will not buy into the lies about marriage that the media and culture are selling them.

> *It's really hard to fight with someone you pray with regularly.*

- Ask for power and creativity to keep finding fresh new ways as a married couple to seek God as your "One."

- Commit to God that you will accept the challenge to pray together as a couple daily.

BETWEEN SESSIONS

LEAVING THINGS BEHIND

God offers you a fresh start in your marriage "from this day forward." The apostle Paul gave this simple exhortation: "One thing I do: Forgetting what lies behind and reaching forward to what lies ahead ..." (Philippians 3:13). We all have past hurts and failures that can paralyze us in the future if we let them.

Take time in the coming week to make a mental list of things you have done or said in your marriage that you wish you had not. You might even think of things you wished you had done but have never gotten around to. Now, bring each of these to the foot of the cross and confess them to Jesus, leave them there, and begin a new day. Accept his grace, start fresh, and live in a new way.

If there are negative patterns from the past, change them in the future with the help and power of God, the One who is first in your life. If there are things you always meant to do, ask for power to begin taking action and doing them now ... "from this day forward."

DEALING WITH IDOLS

Review your bank ledger and calendar from the past month and reflect on where you spend your money and your time. Prayerfully consider anything or anyone that might have first place in your life instead of God, or might slowly be creeping there.

It's not too late to learn how to do things God's way.

Confess these things to God and repent of them. Change your behavior, schedule, actions, finances, and whatever needs to be adjusted to make sure God is your number one priority and that you are seeking him first. You might even want to contact a member of your small group (men contact men and women contact women); ask them to pray for you and check in with you in a week to find out how you are doing with this commitment.

REALISTIC EXPECTATIONS

Think about how you may have idolized your spouse and ended up demonizing them when they let you down and were not able to match up to your unrealistic expectation. Use the following chart to note a few examples of such behavior on your part. Then, set a goal on how you want to look at your spouse in a way that is godly, balanced, and optimistic.

> *The decisions you make today determine the marriage you will have tomorrow.*

How I Idolized	How I Demonized	My New Realistic Outlook

JOURNAL

Use the space provided (or a separate notebook) to reflect on any of the following topics:

- In what ways do I want to place God in the center of my heart and life?

- Where am I letting people or things take too central a place in my heart and life (instead of God)?

- What is making it difficult for me to seek God with my spouse, and how can we overcome this together?

- What lies of the media or culture do I sometimes buy into, and how I will be on guard to resist them?

- How is my prayer time with my spouse going?

FOR FURTHER READING

As you reflect on what you have learned in this session, please read chapter 1 of the book *From This Day Forward* by Craig and Amy Groeschel. In preparation for the next session, please read chapter 2.

FIGHT FAIR

The question for every couple is not, "Will we fight?"
The answer to that question is an emphatic "yes"
for every honest couple. The real question is,
"Will we fight fair and will we seek healthy resolution?"

WHEN THE BUBBLE BURSTS (2 – 3 MINUTES)

Dan and Monika were in love! They had been married for six months, and things seemed to be going so smoothly. Until the Valentine's Day blowup.

Dan had a busy day at work and forgot to get Monika a card or plan anything special. When he got home that night he was exhausted, so he promised to take her out for a Valentine's Day dinner sometime in the next week or two. Then he flopped into his chair and turned on the TV to catch up on the sports scores.

Tears in her eyes, Monika placed a handmade card and a thoughtful gift on Dan's lap, and then walked slowly to the bedroom where she sat on the edge of the bed and waited. Dan did not come. The details are not the issue, but Monika expressed her hurt, anger, and disappointment in a way Dan had never seen before. She blew up!

Carl and Rosie came from very different backgrounds, but they really loved each other. Throughout their engagement they talked and often laughed about how different their families were. They would often quote the old adage, "Opposites attract!" When they got married, they figured it would be easy to navigate the many differences they knew about and all the others they would discover along the way. They agreed that their home and family would be a healthy merging of family traditions, histories, and idiosyncrasies.

> *All couples fight, but healthy couples fight fair.*

One wedding and one month later, they discovered that it might not be quite as easy and fun as they had anticipated. Carl grew up in a large family that loved family meals. They would all spend more than an hour at the dinner table at least three evenings a week, and the Sunday afternoon meal following church — a major production with food, laughter, and conversations — could last even longer. Rosie grew up as an only child, raised by her mom.

After nine hours at the office and a forty-five minute commute, Rosie's mom would pick up something quick on the way home or microwave a meal out of the freezer.

After four weeks of take-out sushi, microwave meals, and frozen pizza, Carl got angry and explained to Rosie that they had not really had a proper meal since they were married. He asked when she was going to begin making "real meals."

The reality is, every couple will fight. The bubble might burst while dating, during the engagement, or months into the marriage ... but it will burst. This does not mean the honeymoon is over or that the marriage is doomed, only that two different people are learning to become one. As they commit to love each other from this day forward, they *will* have fights, but they must learn to fight fair.

TALK ABOUT IT (4 – 5 MINUTES)

What is one of the craziest or silliest things you ever had a fight about as a couple, and why did it seem like such a big deal at the time?

In marriage, it is often the smallest things that create the biggest problems.

VIDEO TEACHING NOTES (18 MINUTES)

As you watch the video teaching segment for session 2, use the following outline to follow along or to record anything that stands out to you.

The great pancake war! How small things can become big things in a marriage.

The goal in a healthy marriage is to always fight toward resolution.

Three Principles for Fighting Clean:
1. Stop to listen carefully.
2. Guard our words faithfully.
3. Handle anger righteously.

"My dear brothers and sisters, take note of this: Everyone should be quick to listen, slow to speak and slow to become angry" (James 1:19).

Principle #1: Stop to Listen Carefully.

Repeat back what you have heard. Do this with sincerity and with the intention of validating the other person's feelings.

Principle #2: Guard Our Words Faithfully.

"Watch your tongue and keep your mouth shut, and you will stay out of trouble" (Proverbs 21:23 NLT).

In the heat of the moment, always ask two questions of yourself: Should it be said? Should it be said now?

Work on your marriage during non-conflict times. Ask: What are three things I do that bless you? Ask: What are three things I could do that would be an even greater blessing?

Some basic rules of engagement (what we say and how we say it):

1. Never call names.
2. Never raise your voice.
3. Never get "historical."
4. Never say "never" or "always."
4. Never threaten divorce.
6. Never quote your pastor.

Principle #3: Handle Anger Righteously.

"Therefore each of you must put off falsehood and speak truthfully ... for we are all members of one body. 'In your anger, do not sin': Do not let the sun go down while you are still angry, and do not give the devil a foothold" (Ephesians 4:25 – 27).

There are different ways and styles of dealing with anger.

Two critical and essential virtues to navigate anger in a righteous manner: self-control and humility.

The issue of timing: don't let the sun go down on your anger.

Four Signs You Are Not Fighting Fair:

1. *Criticizing:* "You never do what you said you would do."
2. *Contempt:* "I don't even like the person I am with."
3. *Defensiveness:* "It's all your fault."
4. *Stonewalling:* "I'm done; I am so over this!"

We need to get on the same side of the table. We need to get together, look to God, and fight against the real enemy — the devil!

Advice for those who feel that the fight is not worth it: Honor God, honor your marriage vows, and be willing to fight fair and press forward.

> *Never fight with your spouse for victory; always fight for resolution.*

VIDEO DISCUSSION AND BIBLE EXPLORATION
(25 – 30 MINUTES)

1. Craig and Amy talked about how they each process anger differently. Craig withdraws and shuts down. Amy vents and wants to get it all out. What is your style of dealing with anger and moments of frustration in your marriage?

How can your style be unproductive and lead to sin, and what can you do to guard against heading down an unhealthy road?

2. **Read:** James 1:19. What does it look like when a person is "quick to listen" and "slow to speak"? What does it look like when we are quick to speak and slow to listen?

How can these very different ways of listening and speaking impact the anger level of a marital conflict?

3. The first principle Craig and Amy give to help a couple fight fair is: *Stop to listen carefully*. What makes it difficult to listen to our spouse when we are in the middle of a conflict?

What's the best way to be "slow to speak"? Just stop talking.

What tools and practices have you learned that help you become more effective at listening in these challenging circumstances?

4. Craig notes that repeating back what your spouse has said can show you are really listening. How might this tool be valuable and actually diffuse anger if you are sincerely seeking to validate what you are hearing?

Conversely, how can this listening tool create greater tension and conflict if you do it in the wrong way and are seeking to manipulate or frustrate?

5. The second principle Craig and Amy give to help a couple fight fair is: *Guard your words faithfully*. **Read:** Proverbs 21:23. Sometimes the best thing to say is nothing at all. Discuss the wisdom of asking yourself these two questions when you are seeking to navigate a time of conflict: Should it be said? Should it be said now?

Think about a recurring conflict and fight you have as a couple. How might the results of this particular conflict change for the better if you asked yourself these two questions and answered them honestly?

> *Once your words are out there, you can never take them back.*

6. Refer back to the video notes where Craig and Amy offer six rules of engagement for fighting fair. Which of these is the toughest for you to follow, and how can your group members pray for you and encourage you to grow in following this rule of engagement?

Which of these rules is your spouse good at following, and what can you learn from their example?

7. The third principle Craig and Amy say is essential to help a couple fight fair is: *Handle anger righteously.* Anger can surface in a marital conflict in many ways. What are some possible signs that anger is surfacing and/or being expressed in an unrighteous way?

8. **Read:** Ephesians 4:25 – 27. Christians are taught that it is unhealthy to let the sun go down on our anger. What do you think this means, in a general sense? What does this mean, in particular, for a married couple?

Brainstorm ways couples might keep this from becoming a habit in their marriages.

9. According to the video, criticizing, contempt, defensiveness, and stonewalling are four typical signs that we are not fighting fair. Which of these do you think slips into your communication most easily? What can you do to battle this and develop new, more peace-filled communication patterns?

*Fight for the marriage
you both long to have.*

How can your group members pray for you and keep you accountable to work on this area of growth as well as others in this session?

CLOSING PRAYER (5 – 10 MINUTES)

Take time as a group to pray in any of the following directions:

- Ask God to help you see and hear yourself when you are in a fight with your spouse, and invite the Holy Spirit to convict you when you are not fighting fair.

- Invite the Holy Spirit to help you learn to listen to your spouse with growing care and compassion.

> *Don't fight to win. Fight to lose the conflict, and gain a closer relationship.*

- Pray that you will grow in your ability to speak words of blessing and grace to your spouse and that you will learn to refrain from speaking hurtful and angry words.

- Confess to God where you have not followed healthy rules of engagement, and ask for power to fight fair in the future.

- Ask God to help you grow in both self-control and humility in how you relate to your spouse.

BETWEEN SESSIONS

3 + 3 = BLESSING! DO A MARITAL CHECKUP

One of the wisest things you can do as a couple is to invest in your relationship in the times when things are going well. Following is a simple exercise you can engage in as a couple to grow your communication and affirmation of each other.

First, agree as a couple that you want to do the 3+3=Blessing exercise. It is important that both of you are up for it and committed to an honest process of communication.

Second, each of you will take a turn and ask the other this one simple question: *What are three things I do that bless you?* The other will communicate clearly three things that you really appreciate about your spouse. Be honest, creative, and appreciative in your answers.

Third, each of you will ask the second question: *What are three things I could do that would be an even greater blessing?* Each of you will respond with thoughtfulness and graciousness, but this is a time to tenderly communicate some ways your spouse can take a step forward in developing deeper patterns and behaviors of love, care, and respect for you. It is very important that you receive these three ideas without being defensive or pushing back. You

> *Work on your marriage during non-conflict times.*

can ask for clarity, of course, but don't make this an occasion to defend yourself or resist what your spouse has shared.

Finally, each of you will thank the other for their encouragement and honesty and then you will seek opportunities to do the three things they have told you will make them feel loved and blessed.

TAKE THE RULES SERIOUSLY

Take time as a couple to reread the rules of engagement shared by Craig and Amy. Discuss why each one is important and helpful.

Rules of Engagement:

1. Never call names.
2. Never raise your voice.
3. Never get "historical."
4. Never say "never" or "always."
5. Never threaten divorce.
6. Never quote your pastor.

Decide if you want to add any additional rules for the two of you as a couple. It could be, "Let's not bring our parents into the conversation in the middle of a conflict time," or "We will never slam doors, throw things, or be physical during a fight," or "We won't use Bible passages as weapons, but only to guide our conversation," or any other rule that seems helpful for you as a couple.

Our Additional Rules of Engagement:

7. _____

8. _____

9. _____

> *If the two of you can find some way to seek God together, and if you'll commit to fight fair, then we believe that the presence of God can bring healing to any relationship.*

You might even want to print out a couple of copies of these rules or put them in your phone, tablet, or computer so you have them handy as a reminder whenever you face a time of conflict. Be sure to respect the rules and you will find fights more redemptive and less damaging.

PRACTICE ACTIVE LISTENING

Set aside thirty minutes, as a couple, to practice active listening in a controlled setting when you are not actually experiencing tension or conflict.

Each of you will have ten minutes to tell your spouse about an area of your relationship that you would like to see grow or improve. The other person will listen carefully and closely and seek to reflect back what they are hearing. The goal is to show that you hear what is being expressed, understand the other's concern, and care about their feelings. You can reflect back by saying things like:

What I hear you saying is ...

As I listen, it seems like you are feeling ...

If I am hearing you correctly, you would like to see me...

I think I get what you are saying; let me see if I have this right ...

You are communicating your thoughts beautifully; I hear you asking me to ...

I think I get your heart on this topic; you are saying ...

I'm not sure I fully understand what you are seeking to
communicate; can you say that again …

I understood part of what you said, but I need a little help and
clarity on one part of what you are communicating …

After one of you has talked for ten minutes while your spouse
is practicing active listening, stop and take about five minutes to
discuss how it went. What did your spouse do and say that was
helpful as an active listener? Were there any responses that did not
feel natural or authentic? Were there any responses that made you
feel heard and cared for?

Then, switch and have the
other person practice active
listening skills.

> *Even if you don't agree with
> the other person, you can
> still validate their feelings.*

JOURNAL

*Use the space provided (or a separate notebook) to reflect on any of
the following topics:*

- What are some of our recurring conflict points as a couple,
  and how can I seek to avoid having the same fight over and
  over?

- When is it hardest for me to keep my mouth shut and listen?
  How can I prepare to listen better and talk less the next time
  I face that specific situation?

- Which rules of engagement do I have the hardest time
  following? What can I do to have a better chance of
  following this rule next time I face a conflict in my
  marriage?

- What will it look like, in my marriage, to make sure the sun
  does not go down on my anger?

- What are a couple of ways I can bless my spouse and communicate how much I love them during the good times?

FOR FURTHER READING

As you reflect on what you have learned in this session, read chapter 2 of the book *From This Day Forward* by Craig and Amy Groeschel, if you haven't already. In preparation for the next session, read chapter 3.

HAVE FUN

*Without fun, play, laughter, and romance,
the best of marriages can deteriorate quickly
into a joyless business relationship.
In many cases, the responsibilities and pressures
of life can push out the fun without us noticing.
Most couples need to be intentional about
making space for fun and bringing joy
into their relationship on a daily basis ...
for all the years God gives them.*

THAT WAS THEN, THIS IS NOW (2 – 3 MINUTES)

Joy came naturally and fun was frequent. In year one of their marriage, Chip and Darlene seemed to be naturals at making space in their schedules to be together and enjoy the married life Jesus had given them.

Long chats over a cup of coffee were a weekly event. Laughter and prayer seemed to be on their lips each day. They did not always see the world from the same vantage point, but a heartfelt conversation about their differences seemed to iron out the tension pretty quickly. Chip and Darlene were not mushy, but everyone could see that they loved to be together.

Both of them took time to enter the world of the other. Chip had never been into photography, but Darlene was passionate about it. So, once a month they spent half a Saturday taking pictures around their home and community. Darlene used a high-quality camera and Chip used his smartphone, but he was into it! Darlene had never been a big sports enthusiast, but she made a point of talking with Chip about the teams he enjoyed, attended an occasional sporting event with her husband, and even got a bike to ride with him and walked the golf course with him on occasion.

Their solid communication, frequent laughter, and engagement in common interests seemed to lead naturally to romance. No details needed, but Chip and Darlene were passionate about each other on every level. Physical intimacy and romantic engagement were an extension of their love for God and enjoyment of each other. When they felt close to one another, they expressed it in ways that married couples are designed to show their love.

> *Having fun in your marriage should be an ongoing series of current events.*

In year seven of their marriage, the story had evolved, and the picture was not as pretty. Chip and Darlene were busy. They had a four-year-old daughter, a two-year-old son, and were seven months along with baby number three.

Lingering chats over coffee were now replaced by quick gulps as a child was being handed off and information was being exchanged. Laughter was still in the home, but it was more often laughing with the kids, or at them. When tension came up, the idea of processing and talking about it for an hour was a distant memory. A quick argument was often followed by, "Let's deal with this later," and an expectation that both would forget the whole thing by the time they flopped exhausted into bed at the end of the day.

Playtime, common interests, and their half-day photography outings seemed like a distant dream. Childcare, financial survival, and conflict management seemed to be more urgent than a walk together on the golf course.

Romance and intimacy had not died, but their cousin, quick sex, had moved into their bedroom — it just seemed more practical in this season of life.

Chip and Darlene still loved each other. They were just realists. They understood this was the natural way marriage changed when you face time limitations, when you are raising kids, and when the endless demands of life never stop knocking on your door.

But in the quiet of the night, after the kids were down, both Chip and Darlene wondered if they might recapture some of the joy, laughter, intimacy, and fun of the early years in this new season of marriage. Was it even possible?

TALK ABOUT IT (4 – 5 MINUTES)

Tell about a great date you experienced with your spouse or fiancé(e). What made this date so special and memorable?

Without fun and romance, a marriage becomes like a business relationship.

VIDEO TEACHING NOTES (16 MINUTES)

As you watch the video teaching segment for session 3, use the following outline to follow along or to record anything that stands out to you.

Having fun includes figuring out what your spouse enjoys and learning to engage in this as a couple.

Sometimes, as the pressures of life come pressing in, we forget to have fun together ... we don't work at it and make it a priority.

Three Types of Fun that Should Be Part of Every Marriage

1. Face-to-face fun

Beware when technology takes over and we email, text, use social media, talk on the phone, but never get face-to-face.

Beware when face-to-face time becomes a matter of doing family business. Discussing chores and organizing schedules does not qualify as face-to-face fun!

Song of Solomon 7:1 – 4 ... pictures of face-to-face fun.

This time includes intimate and ongoing conversation with details and specifics.

The importance of having a date night (being together just to be together):

- You must **create** and **innovate** this.
- You must **guard** this.
- You must **do** this.

2. Side-to-side fun

Discover and engage in activities you enjoy together.

These can be ordinary daily things or crazy surprising things, but it involves entering into your spouse's world.

Song of Solomon 7:11 ... a picture of side-to-side fun.

Ask the question, "What does my spouse love?" and then learn to love it with them.

Husbands tend to open up to their wives on a deep level at two times: when they are doing an activity or hobby they really enjoy side-by-side, and after they have had intimate physical connection.

3. Belly button-to-belly button fun

Proverbs 5:18 – 20 ... God delights in the intimacy between a man and a woman in marriage.

Men:
- Work on your approach, vary it, be creative.
- Be tender.

- Be romantic.
- Engage in conversation.
- Bring gifts.
- Lavish her with love.
- Find out what she likes and do it.

Women:

- Make an approach … any approach.
- Get romantic.
- Everything looks better in silk than in flannel.
- Play great music.
- Draw a bath.
- Give a back rub.
- Find out what he likes and do it.

Song of Solomon 7:10 – 12 … a picture of belly button-to-belly button fun.

When you're married, fun is not a luxury; it's a requirement.

VIDEO DISCUSSION AND BIBLE EXPLORATION

(25 – 30 MINUTES)

1. What are some of the normal things of life that can get in the way of face-to-face fun time with your spouse? What can you do to be intentional and consistent about making time for face-to-face fun?

2. **Read:** Song of Solomon 7:1 – 4 (also called Song of Songs in some Bible translations, including the NIV). How does this passage give us an example of face-to-face fun? How might a relationship change for the better if both the husband and wife spoke this way to each other, face-to-face, on a regular basis?

3. In the video teaching, Craig talked about a season when he and Amy were so busy with children and ministry that they stopped having their weekly date night, and how it cost them as a couple. Share about a time in your own marriage when good, consistent face-to-face time got pushed to the side. How did this impact your relationship (spiritually, emotionally, and romantically)?

What did you do to get back in the rhythm of making time for face-to-face fun together as a couple?

What advice would you give to a couple who says, "In this season of our life we are just too busy to get this kind of time together. We will get back to this when things slow down"?

> *If you don't guard it, life will squeeze the intimacy out of your face-to-face fun!*

4. Side-to-side fun is about finding activities, hobbies, and passions your spouse enjoys and learning to engage in these together. Tell about a side-to-side activity you do as a couple and how this connects you and makes space for fun together.

5. **Read:** Song of Solomon 7:11. This picture of a couple taking a walk together, side by side, should inspire us to walk into the world of our spouse and engage in what matters to them. What is one activity your spouse enjoys that you have not really engaged in, and how might you walk side by side with them into this area in the coming weeks? If you are open to some accountability, invite your group members to check in and see if you have taken action on this side-to-side fun time. (Note: A side-to-side connection does not mean being fully immersed in these parts of your spouse's life but engaging in a measured and meaningful way.)

6. What excuses have you used (or are using now) to justify not having consistent and quality time together? How can you get rid of excuses and make time to be together and have some fun?

> *Prioritize your schedule.*
> *Quality time together*
> *is crucial for a thriving*
> *relationship.*

7. Belly button-to-belly button fun is about romance, intimacy, and enjoying ourselves sexually as a husband and wife. **Read:** Proverbs 5:15 – 19. In this passage, romantic and sexual love between a husband and wife is described using the image of water. What does this passage teach us about how God sees sexuality and how we should view it?

8. What is the connection between face-to-face fun, side-to-side fun, and belly button-to-belly button fun? If the first two kinds of fun are happening, what impact do they have on the third kind of fun? If the first two are *not* happening, what influence does it have on belly button-to-belly button fun?

9. In the video teaching, Craig and Amy offer some suggestions for husbands to develop their belly button-to-belly button fun times with their wife. Why is each of these important?

- Being creative and fresh in his approach
- Being tender before, during, and after
- Developing a sense of romance in all of life but especially in the bedroom
- Engaging in good conversation
- Giving thoughtful gifts
- Being consistent in love and care, not just when it is belly-button fun time
- Asking, knowing, and doing what she enjoys

10. In the video teaching, Craig and Amy also offer some suggestions for wives as they seek to develop their belly button-to-belly button fun times with their husband. Why is each of these important?

- Making an approach, initiating, and seeking intimacy
- Responding well to romantic overtures
- Seeking to look beautiful for her husband
- Setting the stage (good music, a bath, a back rub) for fun
- Asking, knowing, and doing what he enjoys

Physical intimacy is directly related to your process of growing together, and it can be a good indicator of how healthy your relationship is—or isn't.

CLOSING PRAYER (5 – 10 MINUTES)

Take time as a group to pray in any of the following directions:

- Praise God for his plan of a man and woman being in love and enjoying life together.

- Thank God for the good seasons when fun has been plentiful and you felt very close to your spouse. Pray that some of that joy and excitement will return to your relationship.

- Ask God to help you be creative in how you make opportunities for fun with your spouse.

- Thank God for your spouse's unique interests and passions, and pray for a growing desire to engage in some of these when the time is right.

- Pray for a growing passion for marital fun on all three levels discussed in this session.

- Ask God to help you, as a couple, set clear boundaries and priorities so that you make time for fun in your relationship, no matter what your season of life.

If you want what you once had, do what you once did.

BETWEEN SESSIONS

LET ME COUNT THE WAYS

Take time to read Song of Solomon, making special note of how both the husband and wife are quite fond of listing of what they appreciate about each other. They see the uniqueness of their spouse and love to celebrate it. Write down at least ten things he sees in her and she sees in him as you read this book of the Bible:

What he sees as wonderful about her ...

1.

2.

3.

4.

5.

6.

7.

8.

9.

10.

What she sees as wonderful about him ...

1.

2.

3.

4.

5.

6.

7.

8.

9.

10.

Next, write down at least ten things about your spouse that you really love, respect, appreciate, and notice. These can be physical attributes, personality traits, something about their spiritual life ... anything.

Things I love about my spouse ...

1.

2.

3.

4.

5.

6.

7.

8.

9.

10.

Finally, have your spouse sit down, look them straight in the eyes, and read each item on your list. Read slowly, from your heart, and celebrate your spouse! When you are done, give them the list so they can remember what you said about how much you love them.

> *If you're regularly investing in face-to-face time, your relationship will show it. And you know what else it will show? If you're not.*

REMOVING ROADBLOCKS

Some couples can try to restore fun in their marriage from this day forward, but a level of tension from a past hurt may make it very difficult. If this is your situation, there are some common roadblocks you might want to discuss:

Forgiveness: If you have wronged your spouse in some way and have not confessed this and asked for their forgiveness, this might be a great step to take. Be honest, humble, and specific. Let your spouse know you are sorry and ask for their forgiveness.

Schedule: Some couples have let their schedules get out of control and need to simplify their commitments in order make space to be together. If this is the case for you, begin here.

Replacements: Sometimes a person in the marriage has decided that their spouse will not be a source of fun and has looked to other people to meet this need. This can be in a benign way (through friendships) or in a dangerous way (through a person of the opposite sex who is meeting needs only a spouse should meet). If this is the case, confess it to the Lord and remove the replacement. Commit to find fun and meaning in your marriage.

A NEW APPROACH

Use the lists provided (see questions 9 and 10) and try something new in the belly button-to-belly button fun department. Get innovative, creative, and take a chance. Don't tell your spouse ahead of time; just surprise them. See if some fun ensues!

> *If the grass looks greener somewhere else, it's time to water your own yard. Invest in the marriage that God has given you.*

JOURNAL

Use the space provided (or a separate notebook) to reflect on any of the following topics:

- What can I do to increase the frequency and fun factor in our face-to-face time together as a couple?

- What is an activity I really enjoy that I would love to have my spouse take part in (on occasion)? How can I invite my spouse into this part of my life?

- What have I done in the past (in the belly button-to-belly button fun department) that really seemed to connect for my spouse? How can I make intimacy more fun for my spouse?

FOR FURTHER READING

As you reflect on what you have learned in this session, read chapter 3 of the book *From This Day Forward* by Craig and Amy Groeschel, if you haven't already. In preparation for the next session, read chapter 4.

STAY PURE

We live in a world where impurity is becoming the norm,
sexual compromise is on the rise,
and sexual temptation is everywhere. Into this culture,
God still calls us to radical purity in our marriage.
As countercultural and challenging as this may sound,
God only calls us to things that are possible . . .
in his strength.

A MOVING TARGET? (2 – 3 MINUTES)

In the iconic TV show, *I Love Lucy*, the cameras occasionally found their way into the married couple's bedroom. Of course Ricky and Lucy were never in their beds. That would have been seen as inappropriate. In the 1970s, TV shows avoided showing a couple in bed together ... even a married couple.

Did you notice something odd in the second sentence of the paragraph above? Did it strike you that Ricky and Lucy were never in their "beds"? The word is plural. That's right, only four decades ago TV shows portrayed married couples as having two single beds rather than one large bed that they shared. There was even a little nightstand between the beds.

From a biblical standpoint, there is nothing wrong with a married couple sharing the same bed. As a matter of fact, God celebrates and rejoices in sexual intimacy between a married man and woman.

The point is that our cultural views of what is normal and normative have shifted radically. Today TV shows portray unmarried couples and even same-sex couples in bed together, or engaging in sexual activities in a variety of places. The new norm seems to be an effort to push all boundaries to a breaking point. The idea of sexual purity is presented as a punch line for a joke more than it is held up as a goal for men, women, and even young people.

> *Purity matters to God. If you're married, God expects you to honor the covenant of marriage.*

Yet God has not changed. He is the same yesterday, today, and forever. The Bible has not mutated or adapted to fit culture's view of sexuality. The call to purity and holiness is just as clear today as it was in 1970, 1570, and the first century. The question is, are we willing to seek purity in a world that says, "Anything goes," "What happens in Vegas stays in Vegas," and, "You have the right to do what you want, when you want, with whomever you want"?

Is purity even possible in our modern world? Can we really stand against the tsunami of promiscuity, pornography, and permissiveness? Can a married couple seek and find purity in their relationship in light of the moving target of morality that seems to be shifting faster with each passing day? We can be assured, with God's strength, it is possible to follow his command to honor marriages and keep the marriage bed pure (Hebrews 13:4).

TALK ABOUT IT (4 – 5 MINUTES)

How have you seen the target move when it comes to our world's view of sexuality and purity?

or

How have you seen Christians and churches change their view on sexuality and purity in light of the rapid cultural changes we are seeing?

> *Our natural bent is toward sin, not holiness. We rarely fall accidentally into holiness, but it is easy to fall into sin.*

VIDEO TEACHING NOTES (18 MINUTES)

As you watch the video teaching segment for session 4, use the following outline to follow along or to record anything that stands out to you.

"Marriage should be honored by all, and the marriage bed kept pure" (Hebrews 13:4).

The reality in our world and culture is that there are all sorts of inappropriate things creeping into marriages, including impurities in what people look at, read, think about, say, and do.

Why is there more impurity in marriages today?

1. Greater access to temptation (relationships, social media, Internet).

2. Lower standards.

3. Fewer safeguards and boundaries.

4. We have a spirit of entitlement. People in modern culture don't want to wait for anything.

5. People are waiting longer to get married (if they get married at all). In fact, many people are practicing marriage without being married and they also end up practicing divorce.

Outward Purity

Proverbs 5:8: "Keep to a path far from her, do not go near the door of her house."

1 Corinthians 6:18 – 20: "Flee from sexual immorality ... Do you not know that your bodies are temples of the Holy Spirit, who is in you, whom you have received from God? You are not your own; you were bought at a price."

Matthew 5:29: "If your right eye causes you to stumble, gouge it out and throw it away."

The idea is simple: Run away from temptation to sexual immorality if you want to stay pure. We should deal severely with anything that would cause us to sin and fight fiercely against anything that would lure us into sexual impurity.

Boundaries: We should all set personal boundaries that help us stay a long way from temptation. These are designed to protect us and our marriage and to help us honor God.

Examples from Craig's life:

- Never alone with a woman except family, under any circumstances
- All computers monitored with reporting software
- Two male accountability partners
- Mobile phone locked down

Examples from the lives of other couples:

- Shared social media so that both have access to everything
- Shared passwords for computer and all possible places of temptation
- Agreement not to watch certain movies or shows
- Accountability partners

Outward purity from a woman's perspective:

- Purity must matter to you ... it must be a high value!
- Stay close to God and seek him personally, passionately, and daily
- Be in Scripture and let God's Word shape your thinking and desires

A word to women:

- Honor your husband at all times
- No long conversations with other men
- No intimate friendships with men
- Have boundaries

Inward Purity ... It Is All about the Heart!

Psalm 119:9 – 11: "How can a young person stay on the path of purity? By living according to your word. I seek you with all my heart; do not let me stray from your commands. I have hidden your word in my heart that I might not sin against you."

The critical place of putting God's Word into our hearts.

As I seek God, pray, and think deeply about his Word, he changes my heart and mind.

God wants to change us from the inside out.

Too often we put the boundary line in the wrong place. Before we commit immorality and sexual sin, we have already crossed lines and committed many sins in our heart!

Matthew 5:28: "But I tell you that anyone who looks at a woman lustfully has already committed adultery with her in his heart."

Three Responses to Impurity:

1. **Defensiveness:** This is about fighting back, justifying, and making excuses. The remedy: Humble yourself and stop trying to defend sinful actions and attitudes.

2. **Remorse:** This is being embarrassed, feeling sorry for yourself, and being upset because you have been caught. The remedy: Pray for a broken heart and a truly repentant spirit.

3. **Repentance:** This is about freedom, transparency, and brokenness because there are no more secrets. It leads to seeking forgiveness from God and your spouse.

In the power of the Holy Spirit, you can achieve a level of personal purity that you do not even know is possible!

VIDEO DISCUSSION AND BIBLE EXPLORATION

(25 – 30 MINUTES)

1. **Read:** Hebrews 13:4. What are some ways that a couple can keep the marriage bed pure as they seek to honor and uphold the value, beauty, and gift of marriage?

2. **Read:** Proverbs 5:3 – 12. What warnings and exhortations in this passage will help us avoid impurity if we listen to and follow them?

What consequences mentioned in this passage might we face if we press onward and embrace a life of impurity?

3. In the video teaching, Craig and Amy list five things they believe open the door to growing impurity in marriages. How do you see each of these growing and impacting marriages, and how can we battle against them?

- A greater access to sexual temptations

- Lower standards for sexual purity

- Fewer built-in safeguards and boundaries protecting us from impurity

- A growing spirit of entitlement that says, "I deserve what I want and I deserve it now"

- People waiting longer to get married, if getting married at all

Impurity is like poison; even just a little poison is too much. It takes only a little to kill your marriage.

4. **Read:** Proverbs 5:8, 1 Corinthians 6:18 – 20, and Matthew 5:29. In what ways can we flee temptation that could lead to impurity?

5. In the video teaching, Craig listed some very specific boundaries he has set for his life to protect himself from temptation and enticement to impurity. He also noted boundaries that other couples have set for themselves. Refer to these in the Video Teaching Notes section, and then work as a group to create a list of five to seven additional boundaries couples might want to adopt. These might include ones you have used before, but not necessarily.

Possible Boundaries to Protect a Couple from Impurity

-

-

-

-

-

-

-

6. **Read:** Psalm 119:9 – 11. How can spending regular time in prayer with your spouse and reading the Bible as a couple help protect you from impurity and/or grow you in purity? Tell about a time in your marriage when you did a great job of growing in faith as a couple, and describe how prayer and Bible reading played a part.

Staying close to Jesus sanctifies us.

7. **Read:** Matthew 5:28. In the video teaching, Craig talked about how we can put the boundary line in the wrong place. For example, we decide we don't want to have an affair, but we allow lustful thoughts to rule our mind and inappropriate fantasies to capture our heart. Why is a commitment to grow more and more pure in our heart and mind essential if we want to stay pure and holy in our actions? What are ways we can grow more pure on the inside?

The seeds of sin are planted long before they bloom into adultery.

8. Share your thoughts on at least *one* of the three responses to impurity.

☐ When a person is caught in an act of impurity, they can become **defensive**. What does a defensive attitude tell us about the condition of the heart (our heart or the heart of someone else)?

☐ **Remorse** is about feeling sorry we got caught or embarrassed about others knowing of our sin. Why is remorse never enough to bring transformation and healing?

☐ **Repentance** is about brokenness, transparency, asking for forgiveness, and seeking to live in a new way by the power of the Holy Spirit. How can we tell when a person has moved beyond defensiveness and remorse and is truly repentant?

You cannot build a life of righteousness on a foundation of sin.

9. What is one step you plan to take toward a more pure and holy lifestyle because of this session? How can your group members keep you accountable and pray for you in the coming weeks as you strive for purity?

From this day forward, make decisions that will carry you far away from trouble. If you are wise, you will close and lock the doors of temptation that you can control!

CLOSING PRAYER (5 – 10 MINUTES)

Take time as a group to pray in any of the following directions:

- Ask God to bring revival and repentance in your community and our world when it comes to the topic of sexual purity. It might seem like a big prayer, but God is able to do more than we can dream or imagine.

- Pray for God to move in the lives of Christians so that we can live distinctively pure lives for God's glory, for our good, and for a witness to a world that needs a new vision of sexuality.

- Commit to set boundaries in your life and in your relationship as a couple. Pray for the power of the Spirit to help you set and live within Christ-honoring sexual boundaries that lead to purity.

- Ask God to give you wisdom and strength to live with such purity that you will honor and bless your spouse by your attitudes and actions.

- Invite the Holy Spirit to show you where you are being defensive or remorseful instead of repentant. Pray for a broken heart over impurity in your life and ask God to draw you to a place of heart-changing, action-filled repentance.

> *Sin doesn't begin on the outside.*
> *It begins in the heart.*

BETWEEN SESSIONS

TEN-DAY EXPERIMENT

Jesus talked about cutting off a hand or gouging out an eye if either causes you to sin. The point of these severe statements is that a person who wants to honor God and live a pure life will be ready to cut off the source of sin-producing images and enticements.

One of the conduits of lust-producing images and thoughts is the TV in your home. As the years pass, TVs are getting larger and the options are increasing. In some places, basic cable service includes over a hundred channels, many of which air programs that most of us don't really want to be pumping into our minds and hearts. Indeed, some of these channels become outlets of soft-core porn late at night. No Christian couple needs that coming into their home.

Sometimes, without knowing it, we lower our standards and allow impurity to creep into our lives.

Try a ten-day experiment of limiting or tracking your TV intake. Here are some possible options:

- Keep a journal by your TV and write down every show you watch as individuals and as a couple. At the end of the ten days, talk about the amount of time you spent watching TV and what viewing choices you made. Pray about this and use it as a time to set some new goals.

- Only watch shows together. This might be very difficult, but you will learn a great deal about yourself and your spouse.

- Turn off the TV. Try a ten-day TV fast and see how you might use that time in other ways.

- Limit yourselves to a set amount of TV viewing per day or for the ten days. Seek to stay within the boundaries you set.

- Try watching shows that you both agree are edifying. For ten days, only watch programming that brings something good, valuable, or God-honoring into your home and hearts. You might have some very interesting conversations about what qualifies as an "edifying" show.

SETTING BOUNDARIES AS A COUPLE

Using the list from Craig's video teaching as well as the additional boundaries you came up with as a group in question 5, form a set of boundaries you want to use as a couple. Commit to following these for a month, and then decide if you want to continue with these values or adjust them in some way.

Our Boundaries to Protect Us as a Couple from Impurity

-

-

-

-

-

> *Do whatever you have to do right now to protect yourself later. Shore up your defenses for those moments of weakness. Block every path to impurity.*

THE POWER OF SCRIPTURE AND PRAYER

In the video teaching, Amy talked about how staying connected to God as individuals and as a couple is one of the best ways to battle impurity. Commit to reading one chapter of Proverbs each day for the coming month. After you read the chapter together, identify one or two lessons you learn, and pray as a couple about these ideas and how you can incorporate them into your life together as a married couple.

> *We need to allow God to transform our hearts, so that we can live purely from the inside out and not the sin-side out.*

JOURNAL

Use the space provided (or a separate notebook) to reflect on any of the following topics:

- What can I do to honor my marriage and keep our bed pure?
- Where do I need to keep my path from potentially being tempted toward impurity?
- If I have a hard time setting boundaries and staying within them, what is causing me to avoid helpful and life-giving boundaries?
- How can I connect more closely with God on my own and with my spouse?
- When are times I tend to get defensive, and how can I live with a more repentant and broken heart?

FOR FURTHER READING

As you reflect on what you have learned in this session, read chapter 4 of the book *From This Day Forward* by Craig and Amy Groeschel, if you haven't already. In preparation for the next session, read chapter 5 and the conclusion.

NEVER GIVE UP

*We live in a disposable culture where giving up has
become a lifestyle and quitting has become an art form.
Christian couples must determine,
in the depths of their hearts,
that they will never give up on their marriage,
no matter how hard things get.*

NEVER, NEVER, NEVER GIVE UP! (2 MINUTES)

One of the most famous communicators in history was Winston Churchill. In a time of war and intense strife, he used words to uplift, empower, and move people and nations to stand against the invasion of the Nazi forces and the desire of Adolf Hitler to rule the world.

Churchill was known for taking simple words and phrases to inspire people to heroic action. In one speech, given on October 29, 1941, he said, "Never, never — in nothing great or small, large or petty — never give in except to convictions of honor and good sense."

Never give in.

Never give up.

Stand strong with deep conviction.

Be willing to suffer and even give your life for what matters most.

These words seem almost strange in a time and culture where more and more things are becoming disposable. People give up all the time. When things get tough, when the road is hard, when the pressure is on, many people simply walk away.

Sadly, commitment to marriage has become one of those things lost and left in the wake of an increasingly throwaway culture. Things do get tough in marriages … always! Marriage demands sacrifice and humility. Every couple will face hard days and conflict along the way.

The question for couples is not, Will we experience loss, pain, struggle, disagreement, and hardship in our marriage? The real issue is, Will we stand strong no matter what we face; will we look to God to sustain us; and will we commit to never, never, never give up?

> *You can't do anything to change your spouse, but you can change you. You can do everything you can do to not give up.*

TALK ABOUT IT (4 – 5 MINUTES)

What are the attitudes and outlooks on life that cause so many couples to walk away from each other?

> *To get divorced because you've run out of love is like selling your car because you've run out of gas.*

VIDEO TEACHING NOTES (18 MINUTES)

As you watch the video teaching segment for session 5, use the following outline to follow along or to record anything that stands out to you.

Too often we see marriage as a **contract**. The attitude is, "If you do your part, I'll do mine. But if you don't do your part, I don't have to do mine."

A contract limits my responsibilities and increases my rights.

The reality is, marriage is a **covenant** with God and each other. It is a binding agreement.

A covenant increases my responsibility and decreases my rights.

When we run out of love, forgiveness, and energy to care, this is when God is ready to provide the things we do not have.

We can't say we love God but hate our spouse (1 John 4:19 – 21).

The Principles of Sowing and Reaping (Galatians 6:7 – 9):

You reap __what__ you sow.

- Women are multipliers.
- If you really want your marriage to be different, plant different seeds.

You reap <u>where</u> you sow.

- We need to be honest about where we are investing and putting our energy, effort, and passion.
- It takes both of us, as one, to make our marriage work.

How to Make Your Marriage Be as Good as It Can Be:

We have to agree we are in this together.

We need to believe our marriage is worth fighting for.

We must remember that we are empowered when we understand that we are in a covenant relationship and not a legal contract.

We commit to make our marriage great and not be content with just hanging in there.

We need to commit that we will:

- Seek God.
- Fight fair.
- Have fun.
- Stay pure.
- Never give up!

As you build a strong and God-honoring marriage, God will give you a testimony.

If you don't like what you're getting, look at what you have been giving.

VIDEO DISCUSSION AND BIBLE EXPLORATION

(25 – 30 MINUTES)

1. What are some common indicators that we are seeing marriage as a contract and not a covenant?

What attitudes and actions will be evident in our marriage when we really do see it as a covenant and not a contract?

Marriage is not a contract; it's a covenant.

2. Tell about a time when you ran out of the ability to love, forgive, or really care for your spouse in your own power. How did God show up and give you a surplus of the love you needed?

3. **Read:** 1 John 4:19 – 21. How has God loved us, and why is a deep awareness of God's love essential if we are going to love others, including our spouse?

4. If we claim that we love God, but we also declare that we can't seem to love our spouse, what does this say about our understanding of God's love?

> *When you don't have any love left to give, let God love through you.*

5. **Read:** Galatians 6:7 – 9. Look back at your marriage and tell about a time when you and your spouse sowed good seed into your relationship. What harvest did this bring?

Tell about a time when you were unwise and sowed bad seed into your marriage, and explain some of the unhealthy consequences that followed.

The harvest you get depends on the seeds you plant. You reap what you sow.

6. As a group, come up with a list of ten good seeds (attitudes and actions) that anyone can sow into their marriage and be confident they will bring a good harvest.

-

-

-

-

-

-

-

-

-

Which one of these seeds will you seek to sow into your marriage in the coming weeks, and what practical steps will you take to start sowing?

7. Where are some places we can spend a lot of time sowing seeds other than our marriage? (These don't necessarily have to be bad places, and sometimes they are even valuable investments, but they are places that can take focus time away from our marriage relationship.)

How can we make sure we are not investing too much time and energy in these places and pursuits?

8. It is not enough to just hang in there and be content with a mediocre marriage. What are signs that we are becoming content with surviving in marriage rather than growing a healthy and God-honoring relationship with our spouse?

Your marriage is as good as you've decided it will be.

9. If you have a testimony about how you have worked on your marriage and not given up (even in a hard time), share this with your group. How has God shown up, healed, brought hope, or strengthened you along the way?

> *The only way iron can sharpen iron is if your differences are constantly rubbing against each other.*

10. What are ways we can ensure we are investing the proper amount of time, energy, and focus in sowing good seed into our marriage relationship?

What is one practical step you can take to sow more good seed into your marriage, and how can your group members pray for you and support you in this pursuit?

> *Relational drift happens if we don't commit to regularly sharing our lives as a couple.*

CLOSING PRAYER (5 – 10 MINUTES)

Take time as a group to pray in any of the following directions:

- Ask God to help you see your marriage as a covenant in which you are willing to increase your responsibilities and decrease your rights.

- Confess those times when you have demanded your rights and shirked your responsibilities because you saw your marriage as a contract.

- Invite the Holy Spirit to fill you with love, forgiveness, and kindness in the parts of your heart and life where your tank is running low.

- Ask God to grow your love for him so that your love for your spouse is a natural overflow of your love for God (and God's love for you).

- Pray for wisdom and power to sow more and more good seed into your marriage.

- Ask God to help you spend more time focusing on your marriage than you ever have before.

- Invite the Lord to give you a holy discontent with a marriage that is simply surviving. Pray for a great marriage that honors God and blesses your spouse.

If your marriage relationship has slipped to the point where you feel like your spouse is your enemy, then you should pray for it all the more.

IN THE COMING DAYS

COVENANT REFLECTIONS

When we understand that marriage is a covenant established and honored by God, we stop demanding our rights and commit to love, serve, and sacrifice in the power of Jesus. Take time to write down some of the ways you are going to seek to do this:

In the coming month, I will seek to decrease demanding that things be my way by doing (or no longer doing) the following things:

-
-
-

In the coming month, I will seek to increase my responsibilities and service in my marriage by doing the following things:

-
-
-

Regardless of how you feel, you do what's right.

If you are feeling bold and truly committed to take the actions you just noted, contact a couple of your group members (if you are a man, contact men; if you are a woman, contact women) and invite them to pray for you and hold you accountable.

If you want to take this exercise up a notch, make your spouse aware of *one* action item from each of your lists. Let your spouse know you will be seeking to grow in this area in the coming weeks. Ask them to pray for you.

MULTIPLIER BLESSING

In the video teaching, Craig talked about how women multiply. They have a unique ability to take what they are given and make something wonderful out of it (a home, a meal, a child, and so much more). Husbands, write a letter to your wife (or tell her face-to-face) how thankful you are for the many ways she has multiplied things that now bless you, your family, and others. Identify at least three things your wife has multiplied and let her know that you notice, are amazed, and thank God for how he works in and through her.

THE POWER OF REVIEW

Spend some time as a couple reviewing the five commitments you learned about in this study: (1) seek God, (2) fight fair, (3) have fun, (4) stay pure, and (5) never give up.

Talk and pray about how you are doing in each area. Are there goals you set that are going well? Rejoice in these steps forward and pray for continued strength in these areas. Are there commitments you felt called by God to make that you still have not activated? Agree to get started today.

Set an alarm in your phone or on your calendar that will pop up in thirty days, ninety days, and one year from today. When these reminders come, take out this study guide and walk through the five commitments again, asking the questions in the preceding paragraph.

> *If you are not fully surrendering to God and making him your One, then you can never truly love your two with his unconditional love.*

JOURNAL

Use the space provided (or a separate notebook) to reflect on any of the following topics:

- What are some ways I treat my marriage like a contract rather than a covenant?

- If I believe that my marriage can be as good as I want it to be, what are a few good things I can imagine, dream of, strive for, and invite God to bring into it?

- What new seed do I need to sow into my marriage?

- How can I spend more time investing and sowing good seed into my spouse?

FOR FURTHER READING

As you reflect on what you have learned in this session, read chapter 5 and the conclusion of the book *From This Day Forward* by Craig and Amy Groeschel, if you haven't already.

CONCLUSION

We love the phrase most couples say in their wedding vows: "I promise to be faithful to my spouse as long as we both shall live, *so help me, God.*" We need God in order to love another person unconditionally. We need his help to overlook offenses. We need his help to guard ourselves against all the temptations that lurk around every corner. We need God's help to become more like Christ so we can lay down our lives for each other. Without him, our marriage wouldn't be anything special. Odds are it would end badly, just like so many do.

But by making him our One, he makes us one. And no one can un-one what God makes one. The same can be true for you. You can have the marriage God wants you to have. But you can't have it without God's help.

No matter what's happened in your past, this is a new day. A new chance. A new beginning.

From this day forward, things can be different.

From this day forward, you can find healing.

From this day forward, you can be more intimate.

From this day forward, you can truly forgive as you've been forgiven.

From this day forward, you can become closer to your spouse than you've ever been before.

Just remember: the past is the past. You can't change it. But God can change your future. He can take what the enemy meant for evil and use it for good. What could have destroyed your marriage, God can use to make you stronger and closer and to give you an unbreakable bond.

It might feel like you have too much to overcome. You don't. It might seem like the damage is too great to be repaired. It's not. You might not think you have what it takes. You don't. But God does.

Don't let this be complicated. It doesn't have to be. Keep your marriage simple, focused, and Christ-centered.

No matter what's happened before, you will seek the One with your two. He is your source. Your strength. Your sustainer.

You will fight fair. You don't fight *for* victory; you fight *from* the victory God has given you. Together you will find resolution. And your differences won't divide you; they'll strengthen you.

You will enjoy each other like you once did, having fun the way God intended. Face-to-face. Side-to-side. Belly button-to-belly button.

You will reject the poisons of impurity, and you'll stay pure. You've resolved that even just a moment of impurity is not worth it. Not even a hint.

And because God never gave up on you, you will never give up on him or on your marriage.

From this day forward.

From This Day Forward

Five Commitments to Fail-Proof Your Marriage

Craig and Amy Groeschel

You know the stats, and they are horrifying. Fifty percent of marriages don't make it. With those kinds of odds, is it even possible to have a great marriage? Craig Groeschel insists it is so, but not if you approach it like everyone else does.

In this groundbreaking new book, *New York Times* bestselling author and pastor Craig Groeschel and his wife Amy show engaged and married couples how to conquer the odds in a culture where "I do" doesn't necessarily mean forever. This book will help you find the joy, passion, and strength of a marriage built by God. Craig and Amy present the five commitments all spouses need to make in order to absolutely fail-proof their marriage. Starting right now—from this day forward.

1. Seek God
2. Fight fair
3. Have fun
4. Stay pure
5. Never give up

If readers earnestly choose to do all five of these things, they'll discover a richer, deeper, more authentic relationship and a more rewarding and passionate love life.

Available in stores and online!

Fight

Winning the Battles That Matter Most

Craig Groeschel

Author and pastor Craig Groeschel helps you uncover who you really are — a man created in the image of God with a warrior's heart — and how to fight the good fight for what's right. You will find the strength to fight the battles you know you need to fight — the ones that determine the state of your heart, the quality of your marriage, and the spiritual health of your family.

Craig will also look at examples from the Bible, including our good buddy Samson. Yep, the dude with the rippling biceps, hippie hair, and a thing for Delilah. You may be surprised how much we have in common with this guy. By looking at his life, you'll learn how to defeat the demons that make strong men weak. You'll become who God made you to be:

A man who knows how to fight for what's right.

And don't you dare show up for this fight unarmed. Learn how to fight with faith, with prayer, and with the Word of God

It's time to fight like a man. For God's Sake, FIGHT.

Small Group Curriculum Also Available:
• 5-Session DVD
• Study Guide
• Study Guide with DVD

Available in stores and online!

Altar Ego

Becoming Who God Says You Are

Craig Groeschel

You are NOT who you think you are. In fact, according to bestselling author Craig Groeschel, you need to take your idea of your own identity, lay it down on the altar, and sacrifice it. Give it to God. Offer it up.

Why? Because you are who GOD says you are. And until you've sacrificed your broken concept of your identity, you won't become who you are meant to be.

When we place our false labels and self-deception on the altar of God's truth, we discover who we really are as his sons and daughters. Instead of an outward-driven, approval-based ego, we learn to live with an "altar" ego, God's vision of who we are becoming.

Discover how to trade in your broken ego and unleash your altar ego to become a living sacrifice. Once we know our true identity and are growing in Christlike character, then we can behave accordingly, with bold behavior, bold prayers, bold words, and bold obedience.

Altar Ego reveals who God says you are, and then calls you to live up to it.

Small Group Curriculum Also Available:
• 5-Session DVD
• Study Guide
• Study Guide with DVD

Available in stores and online!

More Popular DVD Studies from Craig Groeschel

Soul Detox

Sessions include:
1. *Lethal Language:* Experiencing the Power of Life-Giving Words
2. *Scare Pollution:* Unlocking the Chokehold of Fear
3. *Radioactive Relationships:* Loving Unhealthy People without Getting Sick
4. *Septic Thoughts:* Overcoming Our False Beliefs
5. *Germ Warfare:* Cleansing Our Lives of Cultural Toxins

Weird

Sessions include:
1. *The God Kind of Weird*
2. *It's Time to Be Weird*
3. *Weird That Money Can't Buy*
4. *Pleasing God Is Weird*
5. *Weird Makes You Truly Sexy*
6. *The Weirdest Blessing Possible*

The Christian Atheist

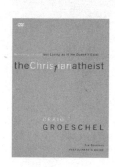

Sessions include:
1. *When You Believe in God but Don't Really Know Him*
2. *When You Believe in God but Don't Think He's Fair*
3. *When You Believe in God but Aren't Sure He Loves You*
4. *When You Believe in God but Trust More in Money*
5. *When You Believe in God but Pursue Happiness at Any Cost*
6. *When You Believe in God but Don't Want to Go Overboard*